GW00322660

# Teddy Bear
# Knits

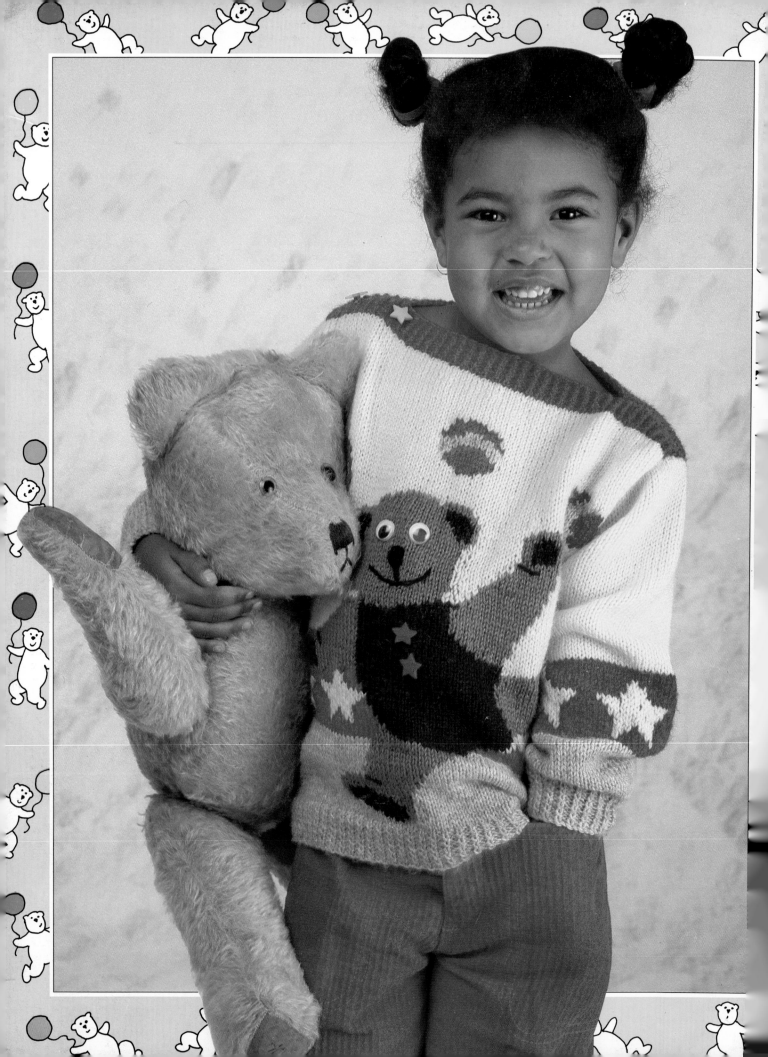

# MO SMITH

# Teddy Bear Knits

**DK**

Dorling Kindersley · London

# Dedication

*This book is dedicated to my husband, Ray, and my children, Andrew and Deborah.*

*It is written in appreciation of the Westminster Hospital and will help support the Andrew Bostic Fund, which was begun to help finance bone marrow transplants.*

*Thanks go especially to my mother, Kathleen Francis and my sister, Yvonne Gale for all their help with the knitting of the sweaters.*

DESIGN: Bridgewater Associates

EDITORIAL: Amy Carroll

MODEL PHOTOGRAPHY: Fiona Pragoff

PHOTOGRAPHY ART DIRECTION: Michele Walker

STILL LIFE PHOTOGRAPHY: Larry Bray

ILLUSTRATION: Katy Sleight

First published in Great Britain in 1987 by
Dorling Kindersley Limited,
9 Henrietta Street, London WC2E 8PS
Second impression 1987
Third impression 1988
Copyright © 1987 by Dorling Kindersley Limited
Story and design of garments copyright
© 1987 Mo Smith

All rights reserved. No part of this publication
may be reproduced, stored in a retrieval system
or transmitted in any form or by any means,
electronic, mechanical, photocopying, recording
or otherwise, without the prior written
permission of the copyright owner.
Printed in Hong Kong

British Library Cataloguing in Publication
Data
Smith, Mo
  Teddy bear knits.
  1. Sweaters 2. Children's clothing
  3. Knitting – Patterns
  I. Title
  646.4'5406   TT825

ISBN 0-86318-229-1

# Bear in Mind

This is a knitting book and story book combined. In it are 16 sweater patterns which highlight the key moments in Jed, our hero's, search for the rainbow, and the happiness it represents. I hope that you will enjoy reading the story to your children and making the sweaters, as much as I think your children will enjoy wearing them.

**MAKING THE SWEATERS** As you read through the book you will notice the sweater designs each have a separate pattern chart; these either precede or follow the story.

A *"Bear Essentials"* box gives specific instructions for each design – the colours used in ribs, sleeves, neckband and back; notes on special embroidery; the yarns used, plus a chart giving numbers of balls for the different sizes; and a selection of appropriate buttons.

● The sweaters feature two different necklines – a crew neck and a slash neck – basic instructions for both styles are given on page 63. All the sweaters have been designed using Sirdar's Country Style Double Knitting. A suggested alternative is Hayfield Grampian Double Knitting, and its corresponding shades are given on page 64, along with some useful addresses for obtaining supplies and sweater kits.

● For beginners, or those whose skills are rusty, a basic knitting ted-niques section (see pp.54–62), illustrates everything you need to know to successfully knit up the sweaters.

● One further note – Jed's eyes are safety ones – they have a "lockable" back which makes it practically impossible for them to be removed. Also I've included an extra knitted backing as an added safety measure. However, if you prefer, the eyes can be embroidered as shown in the basic instructions, and of course, the buttons are purely optional.

# Bear Beginnings

Jed awoke with a start to the sound of raindrops on the window. It had been raining for some time and the sun was just peeping through the clouds. Suddenly he became aware of a beautiful curve of colour stretched right across the sky. Red, orange, yellow, green, blue, purple, violet — the separate shades gleamed against one another. They began just behind the house opposite and disappeared into a cloud.

"Is this a rainbow?" he wondered. "And what does it look like close up?" Suddenly he made up his mind. He'd go in search of the rainbow.

## ◆ BEAR ESSENTIALS ◆

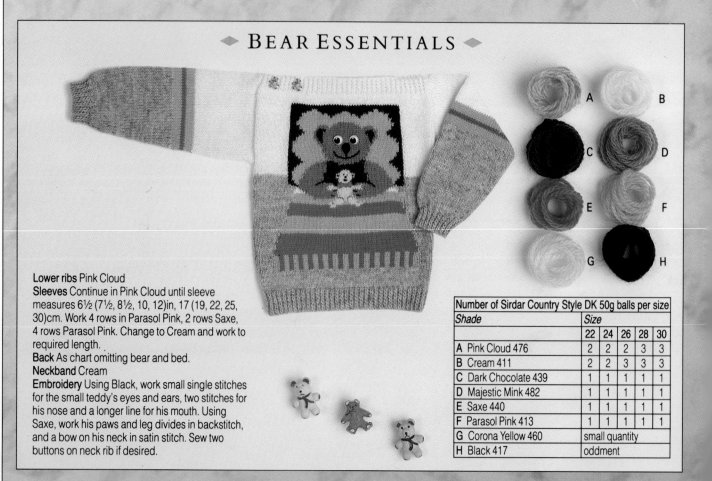

**Lower ribs** Pink Cloud
**Sleeves** Continue in Pink Cloud until sleeve measures 6½ (7½, 8½, 10, 12)in, 17 (19, 22, 25, 30)cm. Work 4 rows in Parasol Pink, 2 rows Saxe, 4 rows Parasol Pink. Change to Cream and work to required length.
**Back** As chart omitting bear and bed.
**Neckband** Cream
**Embroidery** Using Black, work small single stitches for the small teddy's eyes and ears, two stitches for his nose and a longer line for his mouth. Using Saxe, work his paws and leg divides in backstitch, and a bow on his neck in satin stitch. Sew two buttons on neck rib if desired.

| Number of Sirdar Country Style DK 50g balls per size | | | | | |
|---|---|---|---|---|---|
| Shade | Size | | | | |
| | 22 | 24 | 26 | 28 | 30 |
| A Pink Cloud 476 | 2 | 2 | 2 | 3 | 3 |
| B Cream 411 | 2 | 2 | 3 | 3 | 3 |
| C Dark Chocolate 439 | 1 | 1 | 1 | 1 | 1 |
| D Majestic Mink 482 | 1 | 1 | 1 | 1 | 1 |
| E Saxe 440 | 1 | 1 | 1 | 1 | 1 |
| F Parasol Pink 413 | 1 | 1 | 1 | 1 | 1 |
| G Corona Yellow 460 | small quantity | | | | |
| H Black 417 | oddment | | | | |

| | |
|---|---|
| | A |
| | B |
| | C |
| | D |
| | E |
| | F |
| | G |
| | H |

# Teddy Bears' Picnic

Jed had never left the house on his own before but he managed to squeeze out through the open window and slide down the drainpipe. He skipped down the path and stopped at the kerb. There was nothing coming so he marched bravely across the road and knocked on the door of the house opposite.

"Come in, the door's open." Another bear stood there. Jed told him he wanted to see the rainbow close up. The bear took him through to the garden but the rainbow seemed a million miles away. Jed looked so sad that his friend invited him to a picnic. Jed opened a honey pot and soon began to feel better.

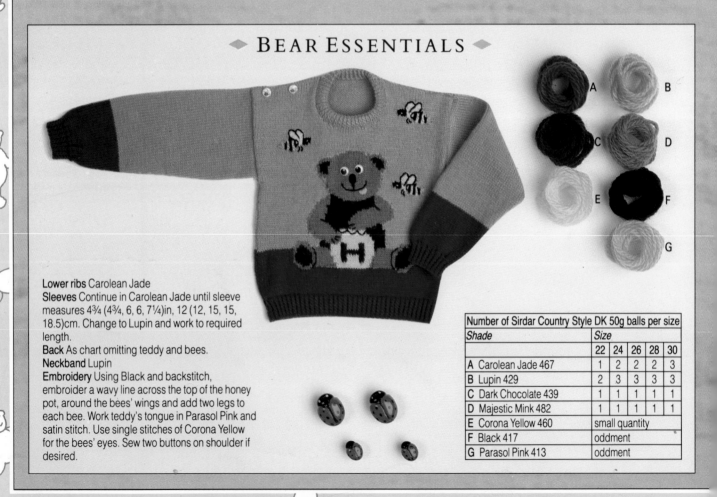

## ◆ BEAR ESSENTIALS ◆

**Lower ribs** Carolean Jade
**Sleeves** Continue in Carolean Jade until sleeve measures 4¾ (4¾, 6, 6, 7¼)in, 12 (12, 15, 15, 18.5)cm. Change to Lupin and work to required length.
**Back** As chart omitting teddy and bees.
**Neckband** Lupin
**Embroidery** Using Black and backstitch, embroider a wavy line across the top of the honey pot, around the bees' wings and add two legs to each bee. Work teddy's tongue in Parasol Pink and satin stitch. Use single stitches of Corona Yellow for the bees' eyes. Sew two buttons on shoulder if desired.

| Number of Sirdar Country Style DK 50g balls per size | | | | | |
|---|---|---|---|---|---|
| Shade | Size | | | | |
| | 22 | 24 | 26 | 28 | 30 |
| A  Carolean Jade 467 | 1 | 2 | 2 | 2 | 3 |
| B  Lupin 429 | 2 | 3 | 3 | 3 | 3 |
| C  Dark Chocolate 439 | 1 | 1 | 1 | 1 | 1 |
| D  Majestic Mink 482 | 1 | 1 | 1 | 1 | 1 |
| E  Corona Yellow 460 | small quantity | | | | |
| F  Black 417 | oddment | | | | |
| G  Parasol Pink 413 | oddment | | | | |

# The Teddy's Tale

Jed's new friend said he had a special story to tell. "A long time ago, before we belonged to girls and boys, rain came and flooded all the earth. But Noah built an ark and saved two of every kind of animal, including bears. At last, when the rain stopped, Noah opened the doors and shutters of the ark and a beautiful rainbow appeared in the sky. Noah told the animals: "This is a sign that the earth will never be flooded again. From now on, love will be with you always when the sun is shining, and also when it is raining, when you are happy or when you are sad, the rainbow will be there."

## ◆ BEAR ESSENTIALS ◆

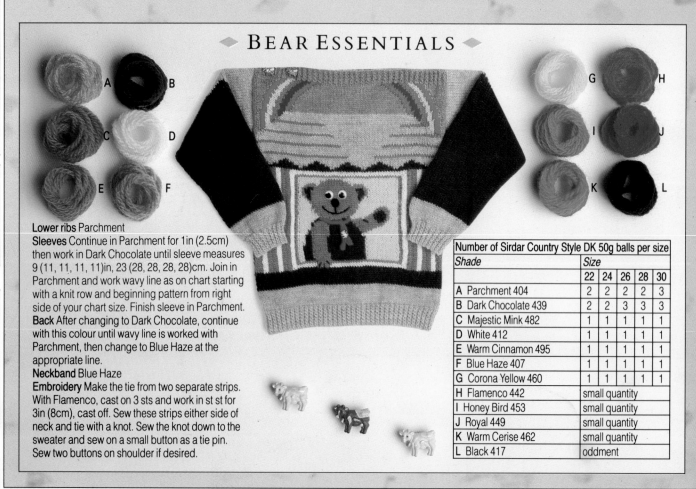

**Lower ribs** Parchment
**Sleeves** Continue in Parchment for 1in (2.5cm) then work in Dark Chocolate until sleeve measures 9 (11, 11, 11, 11)in, 23 (28, 28, 28, 28)cm. Join in Parchment and work wavy line as on chart starting with a knit row and beginning pattern from right side of your chart size. Finish sleeve in Parchment.
**Back** After changing to Dark Chocolate, continue with this colour until wavy line is worked with Parchment, then change to Blue Haze at the appropriate line.
**Neckband** Blue Haze
**Embroidery** Make the tie from two separate strips. With Flamenco, cast on 3 sts and work in st st for 3in (8cm), cast off. Sew these strips either side of neck and tie with a knot. Sew the knot down to the sweater and sew on a small button as a tie pin. Sew two buttons on shoulder if desired.

| Number of Sirdar Country Style DK 50g balls per size | | | | | |
|---|---|---|---|---|---|
| Shade | Size | | | | |
| | 22 | 24 | 26 | 28 | 30 |
| A Parchment 404 | 2 | 2 | 2 | 2 | 3 |
| B Dark Chocolate 439 | 2 | 2 | 3 | 3 | 3 |
| C Majestic Mink 482 | 1 | 1 | 1 | 1 | 1 |
| D White 412 | 1 | 1 | 1 | 1 | 1 |
| E Warm Cinnamon 495 | 1 | 1 | 1 | 1 | 1 |
| F Blue Haze 407 | 1 | 1 | 1 | 1 | 1 |
| G Corona Yellow 460 | 1 | 1 | 1 | 1 | 1 |
| H Flamenco 442 | small quantity | | | | |
| I Honey Bird 453 | small quantity | | | | |
| J Royal 449 | small quantity | | | | |
| K Warm Cerise 462 | small quantity | | | | |
| L Black 417 | oddment | | | | |

Automobear

# Automobear

Jed liked this story and wanted even more to see the rainbow close up. He began to run and jump, as much as his little legs would let him. Soon he was out of breath. The honey in his tummy was going up and down and he felt sick! Poor teddy. Puffing and panting he came to a lane and saw a little motor car. He climbed in, sounded the hooter and began to chug down the road.

It was a beautiful day. The grass looked fresh and green and the buttercups were a bright splash of yellow. In the distance, Jed could see a large striped tent.

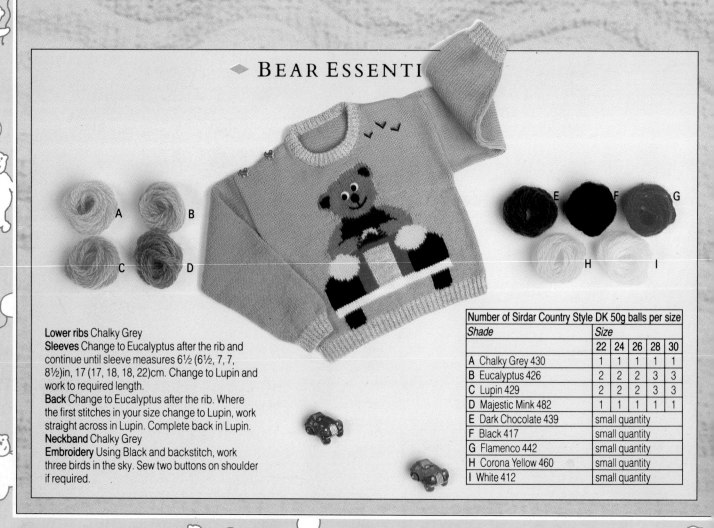

## BEAR ESSENTI...

**Lower ribs** Chalky Grey
**Sleeves** Change to Eucalyptus after the rib and continue until sleeve measures 6½ (6½, 7, 7, 8½)in, 17 (17, 18, 18, 22)cm. Change to Lupin and work to required length.
**Back** Change to Eucalyptus after the rib. Where the first stitches in your size change to Lupin, work straight across in Lupin. Complete back in Lupin.
**Neckband** Chalky Grey
**Embroidery** Using Black and backstitch, work three birds in the sky. Sew two buttons on shoulder if required.

| Number of Sirdar Country Style DK 50g balls per size | | | | | |
|---|---|---|---|---|---|
| Shade | Size | | | | |
| | 22 | 24 | 26 | 28 | 30 |
| A  Chalky Grey 430 | 1 | 1 | 1 | 1 | 1 |
| B  Eucalyptus 426 | 2 | 2 | 2 | 3 | 3 |
| C  Lupin 429 | 2 | 2 | 2 | 3 | 3 |
| D  Majestic Mink 482 | 1 | 1 | 1 | 1 | 1 |
| E  Dark Chocolate 439 | small quantity | | | | |
| F  Black 417 | small quantity | | | | |
| G  Flamenco 442 | small quantity | | | | |
| H  Corona Yellow 460 | small quantity | | | | |
| I  White 412 | small quantity | | | | |

# Performing Bear

It was a circus! But Jed had no money.
What could he do to get inside? Perhaps
the pair of bears in sparkling leotards
could help. Jed told them his problem.
They whispered together then turned and said:
"You're a bear who's on the ball,
No need to mention money at all,
Entertain us, if you please,
And you'll earn your way with ease!"
And they were as good as their words! Soon Jed
was juggling for joy — tossing balls in the air as
though he were a bear without a care in the world.

## ◆ BEAR ESSENTIALS ◆

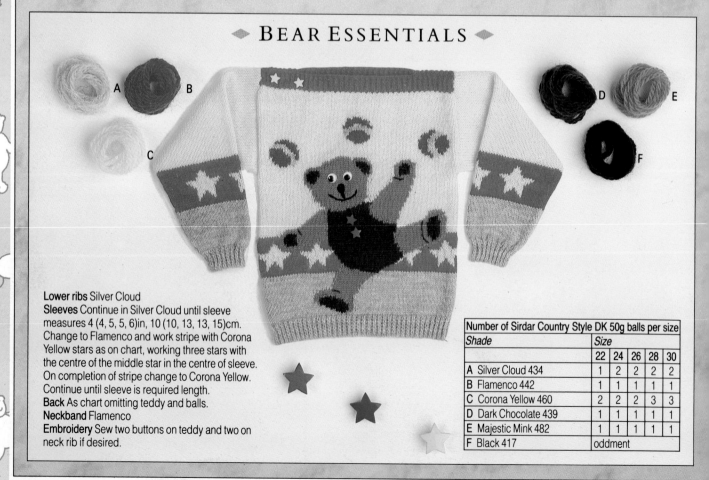

**Lower ribs** Silver Cloud
**Sleeves** Continue in Silver Cloud until sleeve
measures 4 (4, 5, 5, 6)in, 10 (10, 13, 13, 15)cm.
Change to Flamenco and work stripe with Corona
Yellow stars as on chart, working three stars with
the centre of the middle star in the centre of sleeve.
On completion of stripe change to Corona Yellow.
Continue until sleeve is required length.
**Back** As chart omitting teddy and balls.
**Neckband** Flamenco
**Embroidery** Sew two buttons on teddy and two on
neck rib if desired.

| Number of Sirdar Country Style DK 50g balls per size | | | | | |
|---|---|---|---|---|---|
| Shade | Size | | | | |
| | 22 | 24 | 26 | 28 | 30 |
| A Silver Cloud 434 | 1 | 2 | 2 | 2 | 2 |
| B Flamenco 442 | 1 | 1 | 1 | 1 | 1 |
| C Corona Yellow 460 | 2 | 2 | 2 | 3 | 3 |
| D Dark Chocolate 439 | 1 | 1 | 1 | 1 | 1 |
| E Majestic Mink 482 | 1 | 1 | 1 | 1 | 1 |
| F Black 417 | oddment | | | | |

# Tightrope Ted

Now Jed couldn't wait to see the performance. He paid with a pocketful of pennies and found a seat inside. The spotlight was on a monkey dressed in a glittering tutu. She climbed a ladder and began to walk the tightrope. Jed jumped out of his seat. He walked across the ring to the monkey. The audience applauded, thinking Jed was part of the act, so Jed performed for them. He copied the monkey on the tightrope and waved his banners about.

Suddenly disaster! Jed's legs began to wobble, his head started to spin, he crashed into the safety net. Jed's days as a circus star were over.

## ◆ BEAR ESSENTIALS ◆

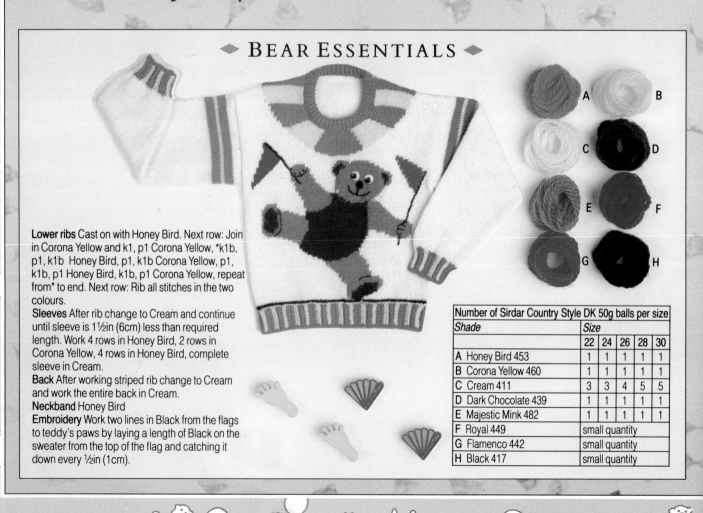

**Lower ribs** Cast on with Honey Bird. Next row: Join in Corona Yellow and k1, p1 Corona Yellow, *k1b, p1, k1b Honey Bird, p1, k1b Corona Yellow, p1, k1b, p1 Honey Bird, k1b, p1 Corona Yellow, repeat from* to end. Next row: Rib all stitches in the two colours.

**Sleeves** After rib change to Cream and continue until sleeve is 1½in (6cm) less than required length. Work 4 rows in Honey Bird, 2 rows in Corona Yellow, 4 rows in Honey Bird, complete sleeve in Cream.

**Back** After working striped rib change to Cream and work the entire back in Cream.

**Neckband** Honey Bird

**Embroidery** Work two lines in Black from the flags to teddy's paws by laying a length of Black on the sweater from the top of the flag and catching it down every ½in (1cm).

| Number of Sirdar Country Style DK 50g balls per size | | | | | |
|---|---|---|---|---|---|
| Shade | Size | | | | |
| | 22 | 24 | 26 | 28 | 30 |
| A Honey Bird 453 | 1 | 1 | 1 | 1 | 1 |
| B Corona Yellow 460 | 1 | 1 | 1 | 1 | 1 |
| C Cream 411 | 3 | 3 | 4 | 5 | 5 |
| D Dark Chocolate 439 | 1 | 1 | 1 | 1 | 1 |
| E Majestic Mink 482 | 1 | 1 | 1 | 1 | 1 |
| F Royal 449 | small quantity | | | | |
| G Flamenco 442 | small quantity | | | | |
| H Black 417 | small quantity | | | | |

# Bear and Butterflies

But Jed hadn't forgotten the rainbow! He climbed back into the little car and began to move slowly down a hill. "Sput, sput" went the engine. Then silence. The car rolled down the hill and stopped. Jed climbed out wondering what to do. He looked inside the bonnet, but his paws were too big to do anything!

Suddenly a crowd of butterflies appeared and Jed gave chase. They led him to the woods, whirling round and round. Soon he was lost. He felt miserable and very sorry for himself. *Bump*. A pine cone fell on his head. He looked up at the tall tree. Could he climb it and find his way back?

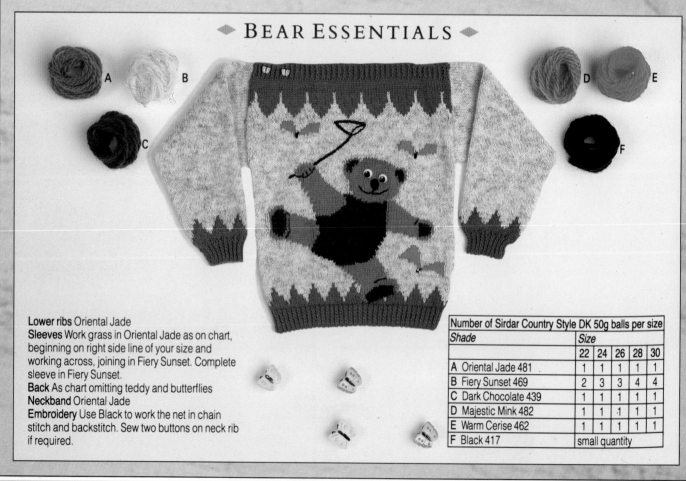

◆ BEAR ESSENTIALS ◆

**Lower ribs** Oriental Jade
**Sleeves** Work grass in Oriental Jade as on chart, beginning on right side line of your size and working across, joining in Fiery Sunset. Complete sleeve in Fiery Sunset.
**Back** As chart omitting teddy and butterflies
**Neckband** Oriental Jade
**Embroidery** Use Black to work the net in chain stitch and backstitch. Sew two buttons on neck rib if required.

| Number of Sirdar Country Style DK 50g balls per size | | | | | |
|---|---|---|---|---|---|
| Shade | Size | | | | |
| | 22 | 24 | 26 | 28 | 30 |
| A  Oriental Jade 481 | 1 | 1 | 1 | 1 | 1 |
| B  Fiery Sunset 469 | 2 | 3 | 3 | 4 | 4 |
| C  Dark Chocolate 439 | 1 | 1 | 1 | 1 | 1 |
| D  Majestic Mink 482 | 1 | 1 | 1 | 1 | 1 |
| E  Warm Cerise 462 | 1 | 1 | 1 | 1 | 1 |
| F  Black 417 | small quantity | | | | |

# Bear and Butterflies

# Unbearable

# Unbearable

It was hard for a housebound bear like Jed to climb a tree but at last he reached the top. In the distance he could see the car and below was the path to take. It was a lot harder finding the car than losing it, but at last Jed was back. He reached inside for the umbrella. "This could come in handy," he thought. And it wasn't long before the clouds gathered and it began to rain. Jed stopped for a while under a tree. His feet were wet, but he kept his umbrella up to stop the drips landing on his head.

## ◆ BEAR ESSENTIALS ◆

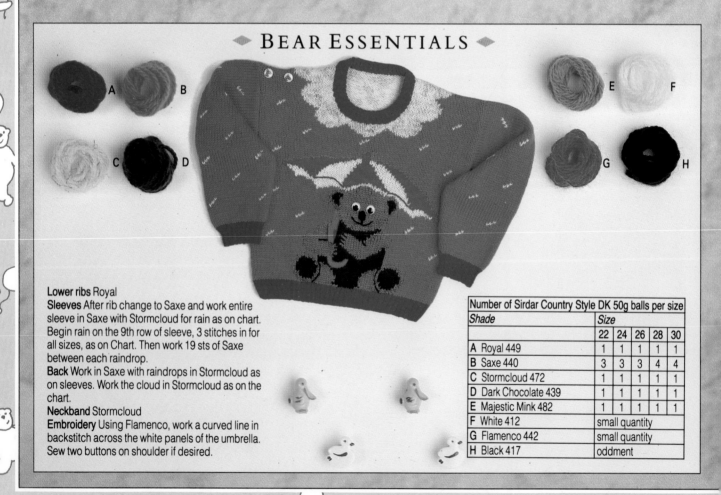

**Lower ribs** Royal
**Sleeves** After rib change to Saxe and work entire sleeve in Saxe with Stormcloud for rain as on chart. Begin rain on the 9th row of sleeve, 3 stitches in for all sizes, as on Chart. Then work 19 sts of Saxe between each raindrop.
**Back** Work in Saxe with raindrops in Stormcloud as on sleeves. Work the cloud in Stormcloud as on the chart.
**Neckband** Stormcloud
**Embroidery** Using Flamenco, work a curved line in backstitch across the white panels of the umbrella. Sew two buttons on shoulder if desired.

| Number of Sirdar Country Style DK 50g balls per size | | | | | |
|---|---|---|---|---|---|
| Shade | Size | | | | |
| | 22 | 24 | 26 | 28 | 30 |
| A Royal 449 | 1 | 1 | 1 | 1 | 1 |
| B Saxe 440 | 3 | 3 | 3 | 4 | 4 |
| C Stormcloud 472 | 1 | 1 | 1 | 1 | 1 |
| D Dark Chocolate 439 | 1 | 1 | 1 | 1 | 1 |
| E Majestic Mink 482 | 1 | 1 | 1 | 1 | 1 |
| F White 412 | small quantity | | | | |
| G Flamenco 442 | small quantity | | | | |
| H Black 417 | oddment | | | | |

# Beach Bear

"To the sea — 5 miles" Jed hadn't known it would take so long when he first set out, but now he was very tired.

At least he was close to a beach. The sea glistened and there was not a cloud in sight. He picked up a towel, bucket and spade and found a quiet spot on the sand.

Jed spent some time building a castle and when it was finished, sat down on his towel to sunbathe. The sun was very hot and he put on his sunglasses. He lay down watching the boats on the horizon wondering where they were going. Before he knew it, he fell fast asleep.

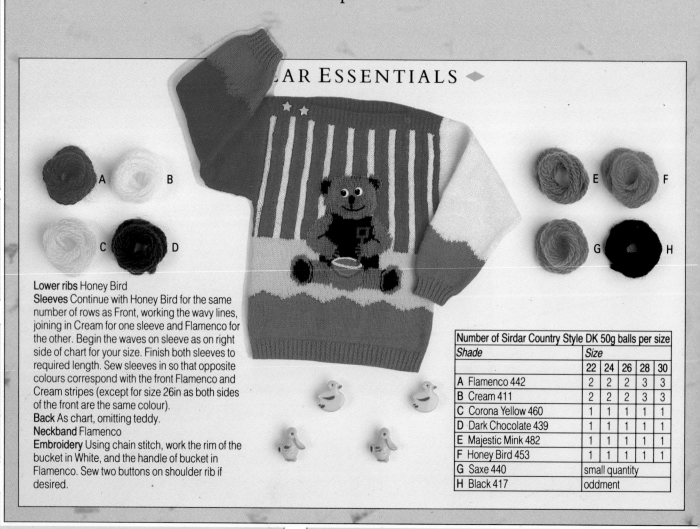

ɛAR ESSENTIALS

**Lower ribs** Honey Bird
**Sleeves** Continue with Honey Bird for the same number of rows as Front, working the wavy lines, joining in Cream for one sleeve and Flamenco for the other. Begin the waves on sleeve as on right side of chart for your size. Finish both sleeves to required length. Sew sleeves in so that opposite colours correspond with the front Flamenco and Cream stripes (except for size 26in as both sides of the front are the same colour).
**Back** As chart, omitting teddy.
**Neckband** Flamenco
**Embroidery** Using chain stitch, work the rim of the bucket in White, and the handle of bucket in Flamenco. Sew two buttons on shoulder rib if desired.

| Number of Sirdar Country Style DK 50g balls per size | | | | | |
|---|---|---|---|---|---|
| Shade | Size | | | | |
| | 22 | 24 | 26 | 28 | 30 |
| A  Flamenco 442 | 2 | 2 | 2 | 3 | 3 |
| B  Cream 411 | 2 | 2 | 2 | 3 | 3 |
| C  Corona Yellow 460 | 1 | 1 | 1 | 1 | 1 |
| D  Dark Chocolate 439 | 1 | 1 | 1 | 1 | 1 |
| E  Majestic Mink 482 | 1 | 1 | 1 | 1 | 1 |
| F  Honey Bird 453 | 1 | 1 | 1 | 1 | 1 |
| G  Saxe 440 | small quantity | | | | |
| H  Black 417 | oddment | | | | |

# Beach Bear

A
B
C
D
E
F
G
H

32

# Ice Cream Bear

# Ice Cream Bear

Jed awoke with a start. The tide had come in while he was asleep and the water was lapping his toes. He looked around for something else to do and noticed an ice cream van further down the beach.

"This is the life," thought Jed, as he licked a huge cornet and felt the coldness sliding down his throat to his tummy. It was delicious. He looked back towards the sea and saw a hot air balloon in the sky. It was the colours of the rainbow. How Jed wished he could have a ride in it. It already had been an exciting day, were there more adventures still to come?

◆ BEAR ESSENTIALS ◆

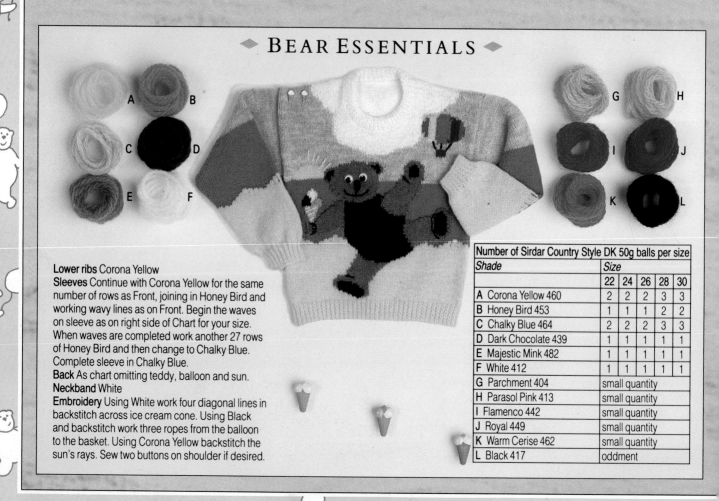

**Lower ribs** Corona Yellow
**Sleeves** Continue with Corona Yellow for the same number of rows as Front, joining in Honey Bird and working wavy lines as on Front. Begin the waves on sleeve as on right side of Chart for your size. When waves are completed work another 27 rows of Honey Bird and then change to Chalky Blue. Complete sleeve in Chalky Blue.
**Back** As chart omitting teddy, balloon and sun.
**Neckband** White
**Embroidery** Using White work four diagonal lines in backstitch across ice cream cone. Using Black and backstitch work three ropes from the balloon to the basket. Using Corona Yellow backstitch the sun's rays. Sew two buttons on shoulder if desired.

| Number of Sirdar Country Style DK 50g balls per size | | | | | |
|---|---|---|---|---|---|
| Shade | Size | | | | |
| | 22 | 24 | 26 | 28 | 30 |
| A  Corona Yellow 460 | 2 | 2 | 2 | 3 | 3 |
| B  Honey Bird 453 | 1 | 1 | 1 | 2 | 2 |
| C  Chalky Blue 464 | 2 | 2 | 2 | 3 | 3 |
| D  Dark Chocolate 439 | 1 | 1 | 1 | 1 | 1 |
| E  Majestic Mink 482 | 1 | 1 | 1 | 1 | 1 |
| F  White 412 | 1 | 1 | 1 | 1 | 1 |
| G  Parchment 404 | small quantity | | | | |
| H  Parasol Pink 413 | small quantity | | | | |
| I  Flamenco 442 | small quantity | | | | |
| J  Royal 449 | small quantity | | | | |
| K  Warm Cerise 462 | small quantity | | | | |
| L  Black 417 | oddment | | | | |

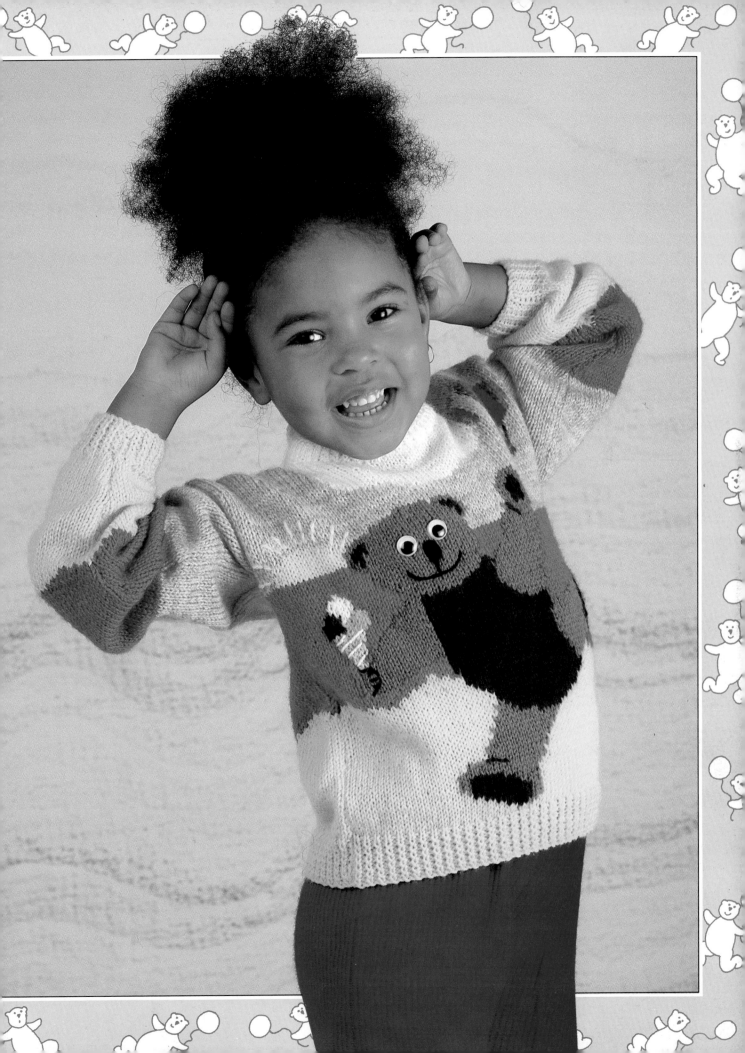

# Barely Afloat

On the sand, just in front of Jed was a bright red boat with yellow sails. He pulled it to the sea, jumped in and started out. It felt great, going up and down, up and down over the waves. He looked back over his shoulder and realised that the shore was quite a long way back. The waves were getting big and a fish leapt out of the water in front of him. Jed imagined himself falling overboard and being swallowed by this fish. A shiver went down his spine. He turned the boat towards the shore and headed back. "Bears belong back on the beach" he told himself.

## ◆ BEAR ESSENTIALS ◆

**Lower ribs** Royal
**Sleeves** Continue with Royal for the same number of rows as on chart, joining in Chalky Blue and working the wavy lines. Begin the waves on sleeve as on right side of chart for your size. Complete sleeve in Chalky Blue.
**Back** As chart omitting teddy and boat.
**Neckband** Royal
**Embroidery** Using White swiss darn waves three rows down from the boat, from one side of the boat to the other. Sew two buttons on neck rib if desired.

| Number of Sirdar Country Style DK 50g balls per size | | | | | |
|---|---|---|---|---|---|
| Shade | Size | | | | |
| | 22 | 24 | 26 | 28 | 30 |
| A  Royal 449 | 1 | 1 | 2 | 2 | 2 |
| B  Chalky Blue 464 | 2 | 3 | 3 | 4 | 4 |
| C  Flamenco 442 | 1 | 1 | 1 | 1 | 1 |
| D  Dark Chocolate 439 | 1 | 1 | 1 | 1 | 1 |
| E  Majestic Mink 482 | 1 | 1 | 1 | 1 | 1 |
| F  Corona Yellow 460 | 1 | 1 | 1 | 1 | 1 |
| G  Honey Bird 453 | small quantity | | | | |
| H  Black 417 | oddment | | | | |
| I  White 412 | oddment | | | | |

Barely Afloat

# Fisher Bear

Jed made a rod from a long thin piece of wood, tied some string to the end and added an old hook that he'd found at the bottom of the boat. He sat down on the end of the pier and threw his line into the water. Soon he felt a great tug on the end of his line and out jumped a big yellow fish! "I've caught one," he shouted to nobody in particular.

The fish wiggled on the end of the line "Let me go" he seemed to be saying. Jed threw him back. "I came out to find the rainbow," he thought, "not make another creature unhappy. It's about time I continued my search." And off he went.

## ◆ BEAR ESSENTIALS ◆

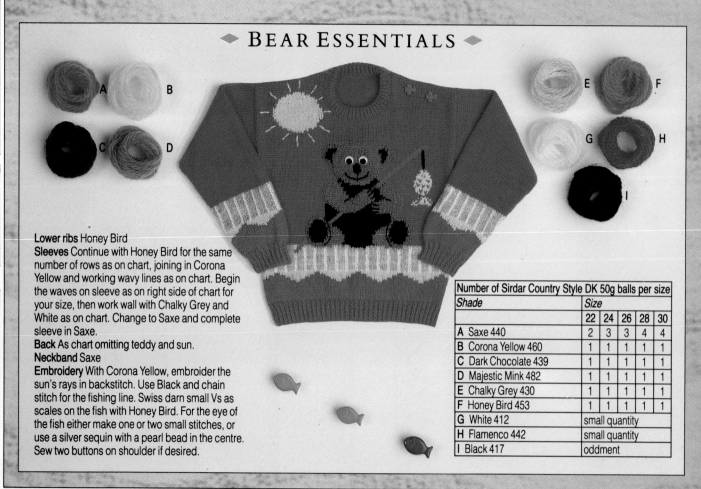

**Lower ribs** Honey Bird

**Sleeves** Continue with Honey Bird for the same number of rows as on chart, joining in Corona Yellow and working wavy lines as on chart. Begin the waves on sleeve as on right side of chart for your size, then work wall with Chalky Grey and White as on chart. Change to Saxe and complete sleeve in Saxe.

**Back** As chart omitting teddy and sun.

**Neckband** Saxe

**Embroidery** With Corona Yellow, embroider the sun's rays in backstitch. Use Black and chain stitch for the fishing line. Swiss darn small Vs as scales on the fish with Honey Bird. For the eye of the fish either make one or two small stitches, or use a silver sequin with a pearl bead in the centre. Sew two buttons on shoulder if desired.

| Number of Sirdar Country Style DK 50g balls per size | | | | | |
|---|---|---|---|---|---|
| Shade | Size | | | | |
| | 22 | 24 | 26 | 28 | 30 |
| A  Saxe 440 | 2 | 3 | 3 | 4 | 4 |
| B  Corona Yellow 460 | 1 | 1 | 1 | 1 | 1 |
| C  Dark Chocolate 439 | 1 | 1 | 1 | 1 | 1 |
| D  Majestic Mink 482 | 1 | 1 | 1 | 1 | 1 |
| E  Chalky Grey 430 | 1 | 1 | 1 | 1 | 1 |
| F  Honey Bird 453 | 1 | 1 | 1 | 1 | 1 |
| G  White 412 | small quantity | | | | |
| H  Flamenco 442 | small quantity | | | | |
| I  Black 417 | oddment | | | | |

# Bears in a Basket

Down with a bang came the hot air balloon and Jed saw the most beautiful bear he had ever seen. He immediately fell in love with her. His knees began to wobble. He just had to stop and talk. He climbed into the basket and told her about himself, where he came from, and all his adventures in search of the rainbow.

"Ah the rainbow . . ." the beautiful bear began. But just as she started to tell Jed something very important, a gust of wind rocked the balloon and Jed knocked against a switch and fell out as the balloon suddenly rose in the air. "Goodbye," he shouted to the beautiful bear. "I don't even know your name."

## ◆ BEAR ESSENTIALS ◆

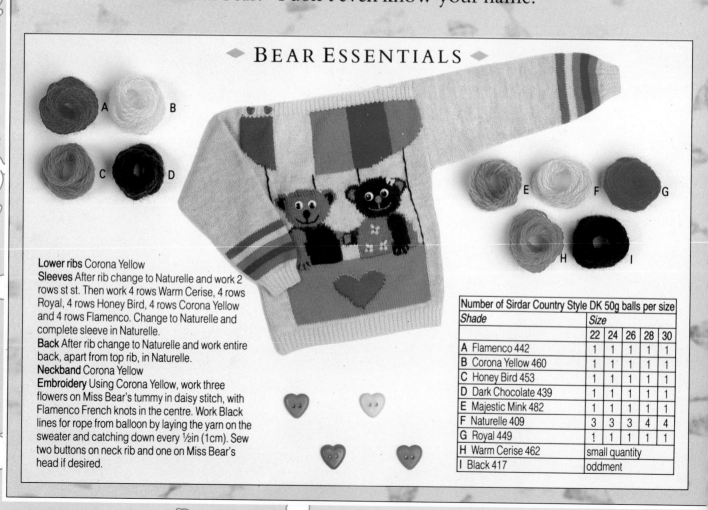

**Lower ribs** Corona Yellow
**Sleeves** After rib change to Naturelle and work 2 rows st st. Then work 4 rows Warm Cerise, 4 rows Royal, 4 rows Honey Bird, 4 rows Corona Yellow and 4 rows Flamenco. Change to Naturelle and complete sleeve in Naturelle.
**Back** After rib change to Naturelle and work entire back, apart from top rib, in Naturelle.
**Neckband** Corona Yellow
**Embroidery** Using Corona Yellow, work three flowers on Miss Bear's tummy in daisy stitch, with Flamenco French knots in the centre. Work Black lines for rope from balloon by laying the yarn on the sweater and catching down every ½in (1cm). Sew two buttons on neck rib and one on Miss Bear's head if desired.

| Number of Sirdar Country Style DK 50g balls per size | | | | | |
|---|---|---|---|---|---|
| Shade | Size | | | | |
| | 22 | 24 | 26 | 28 | 30 |
| A Flamenco 442 | 1 | 1 | 1 | 1 | 1 |
| B Corona Yellow 460 | 1 | 1 | 1 | 1 | 1 |
| C Honey Bird 453 | 1 | 1 | 1 | 1 | 1 |
| D Dark Chocolate 439 | 1 | 1 | 1 | 1 | 1 |
| E Majestic Mink 482 | 1 | 1 | 1 | 1 | 1 |
| F Naturelle 409 | 3 | 3 | 3 | 4 | 4 |
| G Royal 449 | 1 | 1 | 1 | 1 | 1 |
| H Warm Cerise 462 | small quantity | | | | |
| I Black 417 | oddment | | | | |

# Beareft

Overcome by the beauty of Miss Bear and his misfortune at losing her, Jed set off home. He had gone only a little way when he saw a playground. He sat on a swing and swung backwards and forwards, feeling sorry for himself. Suddenly he heard someone say his name. Next to him was another bear. "I've been watching you on your journey," said the bear. "And I want to help you find the rainbow. I've seen it and touched it. It felt so good that I want you to find it too. The rainbow has changed my life and it can change yours also. To find the rainbow, you must go where the river falls over the rocks."

## ◆ BEAR ESSENTIALS ◆

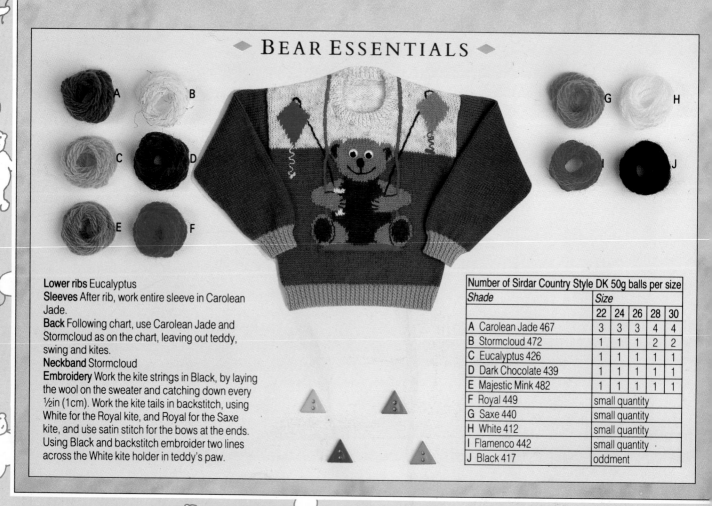

**Lower ribs** Eucalyptus
**Sleeves** After rib, work entire sleeve in Carolean Jade.
**Back** Following chart, use Carolean Jade and Stormcloud as on the chart, leaving out teddy, swing and kites.
**Neckband** Stormcloud
**Embroidery** Work the kite strings in Black, by laying the wool on the sweater and catching down every ½in (1cm). Work the kite tails in backstitch, using White for the Royal kite, and Royal for the Saxe kite, and use satin stitch for the bows at the ends. Using Black and backstitch embroider two lines across the White kite holder in teddy's paw.

| Number of Sirdar Country Style DK 50g balls per size | | | | | |
|---|---|---|---|---|---|
| Shade | Size | | | | |
| | 22 | 24 | 26 | 28 | 30 |
| A  Carolean Jade 467 | 3 | 3 | 3 | 4 | 4 |
| B  Stormcloud 472 | 1 | 1 | 1 | 2 | 2 |
| C  Eucalyptus 426 | 1 | 1 | 1 | 1 | 1 |
| D  Dark Chocolate 439 | 1 | 1 | 1 | 1 | 1 |
| E  Majestic Mink 482 | 1 | 1 | 1 | 1 | 1 |
| F  Royal 449 | small quantity | | | | |
| G  Saxe 440 | small quantity | | | | |
| H  White 412 | small quantity | | | | |
| I  Flamenco 442 | small quantity | | | | |
| J  Black 417 | oddment | | | | |

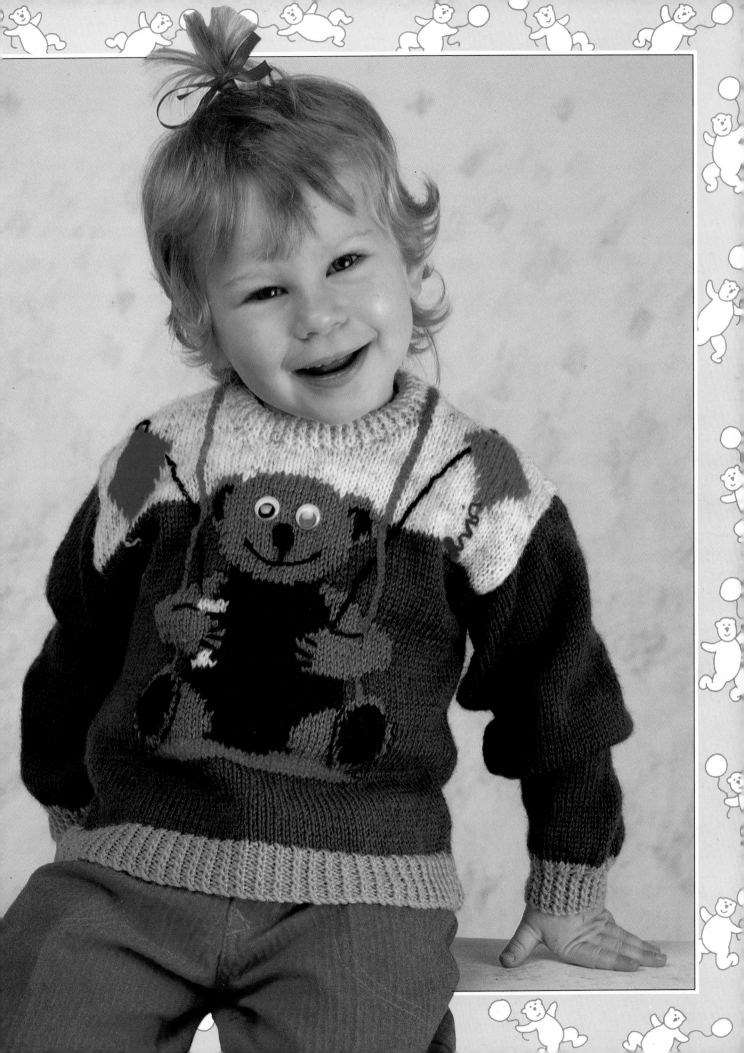

# Rainbow Bear

Without knowing quite how he'd arrived there, Jed found himself at a waterfall close to the most beautiful rainbow he had ever seen. He waded into the water to the top of the waterfall and saw the rainbow right in front of him. He walked out and began to slide down the waterfall, first his feet, then his legs, tummy, arms and head — all went through the rainbow. As Jed passed through the different colours he felt a glow grow inside him. He was bubbling over with happiness. He had found the rainbow, touched the rainbow and now felt happier than he had ever dreamed he would.

◆ BEAR ESSENTIA

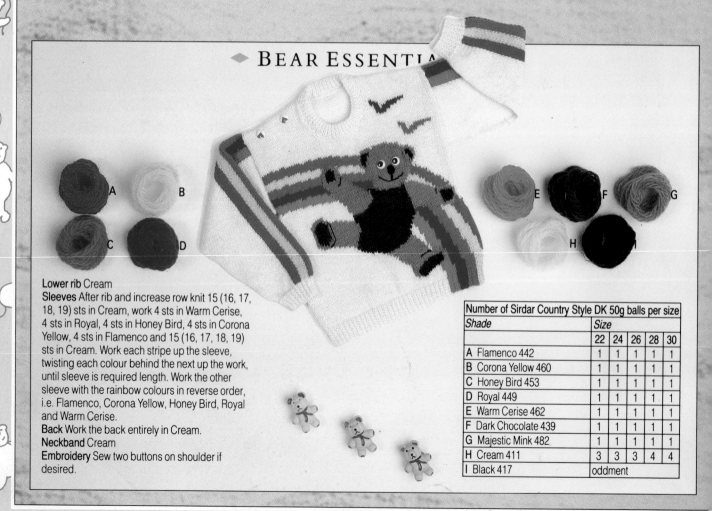

**Lower rib** Cream
**Sleeves** After rib and increase row knit 15 (16, 17, 18, 19) sts in Cream, work 4 sts in Warm Cerise, 4 sts in Royal, 4 sts in Honey Bird, 4 sts in Corona Yellow, 4 sts in Flamenco and 15 (16, 17, 18, 19) sts in Cream. Work each stripe up the sleeve, twisting each colour behind the next up the work, until sleeve is required length. Work the other sleeve with the rainbow colours in reverse order, i.e. Flamenco, Corona Yellow, Honey Bird, Royal and Warm Cerise.
**Back** Work the back entirely in Cream.
**Neckband** Cream
**Embroidery** Sew two buttons on shoulder if desired.

| Number of Sirdar Country Style DK 50g balls per size | | | | | |
|---|---|---|---|---|---|
| Shade | Size | | | | |
| | 22 | 24 | 26 | 28 | 30 |
| A  Flamenco 442 | 1 | 1 | 1 | 1 | 1 |
| B  Corona Yellow 460 | 1 | 1 | 1 | 1 | 1 |
| C  Honey Bird 453 | 1 | 1 | 1 | 1 | 1 |
| D  Royal 449 | 1 | 1 | 1 | 1 | 1 |
| E  Warm Cerise 462 | 1 | 1 | 1 | 1 | 1 |
| F  Dark Chocolate 439 | 1 | 1 | 1 | 1 | 1 |
| G  Majestic Mink 482 | 1 | 1 | 1 | 1 | 1 |
| H  Cream 411 | 3 | 3 | 3 | 4 | 4 |
| I  Black 417 | oddment | | | | |

# Homebound Bear

# Homebound Bear

Jed felt so happy he did a little dance. Underneath the rainbow he began to hop, skip and jump, raising his hands towards the sky. Although he could no longer touch the rainbow, he felt its happiness inside him and knew he would always feel it.

Now he was ready to go home. But how could he get back when he was so far away? Suddenly he had an idea. He took out the balloons that all bears kept for emergencies. Surely they would carry home such a light-hearted happy bear as he was, a bear who was bringing the rainbow's message to all who needed it everywhere.

## ◆ BEAR ESSENTIALS ◆

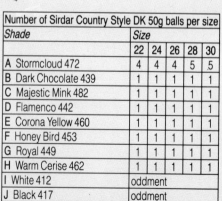

**Lower ribs** Work in stripes as follows:
Cast on with Flamenco and work 2 rows rib, change to Corona Yellow and knit 1 row, work 2 rows rib, change to Honey Bird and purl 1 row, work 2 rows rib, change to Royal and knit 1 row, work 2 rows rib, change to Warm Cerise and purl 1 row, work 2 rows rib.
**Sleeves** After striped rib change to Stormcloud and complete sleeve in Stormcloud.
**Back** After striped rib change to Stormcloud and work entire back in Stormcloud.
**Neckband** Flamenco
**Embroidery** Using Black, work the strings of the balloons in chain stitch. Using two stitches of White work a white cross on the Flamenco, Honey Bird and Warm Cerise balloons. Using the different colours of the respective balloons, outline and fill in a small triangle at the bottom of each balloon. Sew two buttons on neck rib if desired.

| Number of Sirdar Country Style DK 50g balls per size | | | | | |
|---|---|---|---|---|---|
| Shade | Size | | | | |
| | 22 | 24 | 26 | 28 | 30 |
| A Stormcloud 472 | 4 | 4 | 4 | 5 | 5 |
| B Dark Chocolate 439 | 1 | 1 | 1 | 1 | 1 |
| C Majestic Mink 482 | 1 | 1 | 1 | 1 | 1 |
| D Flamenco 442 | 1 | 1 | 1 | 1 | 1 |
| E Corona Yellow 460 | 1 | 1 | 1 | 1 | 1 |
| F Honey Bird 453 | 1 | 1 | 1 | 1 | 1 |
| G Royal 449 | 1 | 1 | 1 | 1 | 1 |
| H Warm Cerise 462 | 1 | 1 | 1 | 1 | 1 |
| I White 412 | oddment | | | | |
| J Black 417 | oddment | | | | |

**BEAR BEGINNINGS**

**TEDDY BEARS' PICNIC**

**THE TEDDY'S TALE**

**AUTOMOBEAR**

**BEACH BEAR**

**ICE CREAM BEAR**

**BARELY AFLOAT**

**FISHER BEAR**

1

## WORKING FROM THE CHARTS

On the graphed patterns each square represents one stitch. The charts are read from the bottom of the chart upwards and from right to left on the first and all odd-numbered rows and from left to right on the second and all even-numbered rows. Therefore, the bottom right-hand corner indicates the first stitch. You must knit all odd-numbered rows and purl all even-numbered rows, following the colours in the squares.

6
4
2

5
3
1

Start **Purl** rows ▶

Start Knit rows ▲

## KEY

1 Pair of 4mm needles
2 Pair of 3¼mm needles
3 Crochet hook
4 Wool needle
5 Needle
6 Stitch holder
7 Tape measure
8 Marker rings
9 Stitch and row counter
10 Needle guard
11 Thread and yarn holder
12 Teddy eyes
13 Scissors
14 Pins
15 Selection of buttons

PERFORMING BEAR

TIGHTROPE TED

BEAR AND BUTTERFLIES

UNBEARABLE!

BEARS IN A BASKET

BEAREFT

RAINBOW BEAR

HOMEBOUND BEAR

# Beginning to Knit

When you begin to work on a pattern placing the first row of stitches on the needle is known as 'casting on'. All further rows are worked into these initial loops. This can be done on one or two needles and the method may be specified in the pattern.

## SINGLE CAST ON

1 Wrap your yarn around two fingers twice and pull a loop through the twisted yarn with a knitting needle.

2 Pull both ends of the yarn to tighten. This produces a slip loop.

3 With the slip loop on your right-hand needle wrap the working end of the yarn around your left thumb and hold it in the palm of your hand. Put the needle through the yarn behind the thumb.

4 Lift the yarn and slide the new 'stitch' towards the slip loop. Tighten the working end to secure the stitch until you have the required number.

## TWO-NEEDLE CAST ON

1 With the slip loop on your left-hand needle, insert your right-hand needle through the loop from front to back.

2 Bring the yarn under and over your right-hand needle.

3 Draw up the yarn through the slip loop to make a stitch.

4 Place the stitch on your left-hand needle. Continue to make stitches drawing the yarn through the last stitch on your left-hand needle.

## CASTING OFF

When you end a piece of knitting you must secure all the stitches you have finished by "casting off". This should be done on a knit row but you can employ the same technique on a purl row: the stitches, whether knit or purl, should be made loosely. When casting off rib, you must use both knit and purl.

### IN A KNIT ROW

1 Knit the first two stitches and insert the tip of your left-hand needle through the first stitch.

2 Lift the first stitch over the second stitch and discard it. Knit the next stitch and continue to lift the first stitch over the second stitch to the end of the row. Be careful not to knit too tightly. For the last stitch, cut your yarn, slip the end through the stitch and pull the yarn tight to fasten off securely.

### IN A PURL ROW

Purl the first two (and all subsequent) stitches and continue as for knit stitch above.

# Basic Stitches

Knit stitch and purl stitch are the two basic knitting stitches. Either one worked continuously in rows forms Garter stitch pattern and worked alternately forms Stocking stitch pattern.

## KNIT STITCH (K)

1 With the yarn at the back, insert your right-hand needle from front to back into the first stitch on your left-hand needle.

2 Bring your working yarn under and over the point of your right-hand needle.

3 Draw a loop through and slide the first stitch off your left-hand needle while the new stitch is retained on your right-hand needle. Continue in this way to the end of the row.

4 To knit the next row, turn the work around so that the back is facing you and the worked stitches are held on the needle in your left hand. Proceed to make stitches as above, with the initially empty needle held in your right hand.

## PURL STITCH (P)

1 With the yarn at the front, insert your right-hand needle from back to front into the first stitch on your left-hand needle.

2 Bring your working yarn over and around the point of your right-hand needle.

3 Draw a loop through and slide the first stitch off your left-hand needle while the new stitch is retained on your right-hand needle. Continue in this way to the end of the row.

4 To purl the next row, turn the work around so that the back is facing you and the worked stitches are held on the needle in your left hand. Proceed to makes stitches as above, with the initially empty needle held in your right hand.

## STOCKING STITCH (st st)

Knitting the first and every odd row and purling the second and every even row produces Stocking stitch when made on two needles.

## RIBBING

A combination of knit and purl stitches, usually one or two knit stitches and then one or two purl stitches, in the same row is known as ribbing. Ribbing is used on sleeve and body edges to form a neat, stretchable finish. It is usually worked on smaller needles than the main body of the garment.

## TENSION

Before starting to make any garment you must make a tension sample in order to measure stitch gauge. You should do this in order to check your individual control of the yarn against the pattern you are following, so that the desired measurements are the same as in the pattern.

The stitch gauge, or tension, is always given at the beginning of a pattern. It is written as the number of stitches, and the number of rows in a particular pattern, e.g. stocking stitch, to a specified size, such as 10cm, using the yarn and needles called for in the pattern. An example is 32 sts and 32 rows to 10cm over st st pattern on 4mm needles.

A variation in tension within a garment will result in an uneven appearance. By knitting the required number of stitches and rows, your sample will reveal whether the yarn and needles you are using will make up into the size and shape you require. When working your tension sample, you must take into account the pattern and the method of carrying yarns across the back of the work (see p. 59).

## DROPPED STITCHES

Occasionally, a stitch may fall off your needle, in which case correct it by following one of the techniques described below. Dropped stitches are often the result of leaving work in the middle of a row.

### PICKING UP A DROPPED KNIT STITCH

1 Pick up both the stitch and strand on your right-hand needle, inserting the needle from front to back.

2 Insert your left-hand needle through the stitch only, from back to front. With your right-hand needle only, pull the strand through the stitch to make the extra stitch. (Drop the stitch from your left-hand needle.)

3 Transfer the re-formed stitch back to your left-hand needle, so that it untwists and faces the correct way. It is now ready for knitting again.

### PICKING UP A DROPPED PURL STITCH

1 Pick up both the stitch and strand on your right-hand needle, inserting the needle from back to front.

2 Insert your left-hand needle through the stitch only, from front to back. With your right-hand needle only, pull the strand through the stitch to make the extra stitch. (Drop the stitch from your left-hand needle.)

3 Transfer the re-formed stitch back to your left-hand needle, so that it untwists and faces the correct way. It is now ready for purling again.

## UNPICKING MISTAKES

Holding the stitch on your right-hand needle insert your left-hand needle into the row below and undo the stitch. Transfer the stitch back to your right-hand needle and repeat undoing until the error has been reached. Correct stitch as for a ladder, see right.

## LADDERS

If a dropped stitch is left, it can unravel down the work and form a "ladder". The easiest way to correct this is to use a crochet hook to pick up the stitches in pattern, although you can try to correct it with your needles.

If you make a mistake in your knitting, you may have to "unpick" a stitch, which can result in a ladder. Pick up one dropped stitch at a time, securing any others with a safety pin to prevent further unraveling.

### CORRECTING A KNIT LADDER

Insert a crochet hook through the front of the dropped stitch. Hook up one strand and pull it through the stitch to form a new stitch one row up. Continue in this way to the top of the ladder then continue in pattern.

### CORRECTING A PURL LADDER

Insert a crochet hook through the back of the dropped stitch. Hook up one strand and pull it through the stitch to form a new stitch one row up. Continue to re-insert hook to make stitches until you reach the top of the ladder, then continue in pattern.

# Working with Colours

When knitting with more than one colour, you will find it necessary to adopt various techniques to keep the back of the work neat and to prevent holes appearing. There are three basic methods of working: stranding, weaving and crossing. Stranding and weaving produce a thicker fabric.

## ADDING YARN AT THE BEGINNING OF A ROW

**1** Insert your right-hand needle through the first stitch on your left-hand needle and wrap the old yarn, and then the new yarn over it. Knit (or purl) the stitch using both yarns.

**2** Leaving the old yarn at the back, knit (or purl) the next two stitches using the double length of the new yarn.

**3** Discard the short end of the new yarn and continue to knit as usual. On the following row, treat the three double stitches as single stitches.

## ADDING A YARN IN THE MIDDLE OF A ROW

**1** Insert your right-hand needle through the first stitch on your left-hand needle. Wrap the new yarn over, and knit (or purl) the stitch with the new yarn. Leave the old yarn at the back of the work.

**2** Knit (or purl) the next two stitches using the double length of the new yarn.

**3** Discard the short end of the new yarn and continue to knit as usual. On the following row, treat the two double stitches as single stitches.

## STRANDING YARN

Use this method for working narrow stripes, and other patterns requiring only two colours in a row. Strand yarn over a maximum of five stitches only.

### IN A KNIT ROW

With both yarns at the back of the work, knit the required number of stitches with yarn A (in this case two), and then drop it to the back. Pick up yarn B and knit the required number of stitches and then drop it to the back. Both yarns should be stranded loosely along the back of the work.

With both yarns at the front of the work, purl the required number of stitches with yarn A (in this case two), and then drop it. Pick up yarn B and purl the required number of stitches and then drop it. Both yarns should be stranded loosely along the front (side facing you).

## WINDING BOBBINS

To help keep different yarns separate when working complicated colour patterns, wind manageable lengths onto bobbins, yarn holders or spools. Replenish as necessary. Or, keep yarns in individual plastic bags secured at the "neck" with an elastic band.

## WEAVING YARN

This method should be used when you are working large pattern repeats, for patterns requiring three or more colours, and when yarn has to be carried over more than five stitches.

### IN A KNIT ROW
1 Hold yarn A in your right hand and yarn B in your left hand to the back of the work.

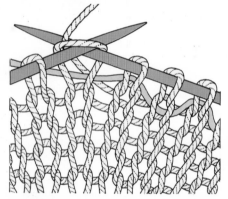

2 Knit one stitch with yarn A and, at the same time, bring yarn B below yarn A. When yarn B is being used, weave yarn A as above.

### IN A PURL ROW
1 Hold yarn A in your right hand and yarn B in your left hand to the front of the work.

2 Purl one stitch with yarn A but this time bring yarn B below yarn A. When yarn B is being used, weave yarn A as above.

## CROSSING COLOURS

Use this method for working solid blocks of colour. When crossing colours each colour is kept as a separate ball or on a bobbin and is not taken across the work. Rather, the yarns are crossed at the join. Follow the instructions below for vertical colour patterns as well, but cross the colours on every row.

### IN A KNIT ROW FOR A DIAGONAL STRIPE TO THE RIGHT
Cross yarn A in front of yarn B and drop it to the back. Knit the first stitch on your left-hand needle using yarn B. On the return row the yarns will automatically loop together.

### IN A PURL ROW FOR A DIAGONAL STRIPE TO THE LEFT
Pick up yarn B in front of yarn A and use it to purl the next stitch on your left-hand needle. On the return row, the yarns will automatically loop together.

## CHECKING YOUR TECHNIQUE

### WEAVING
If you have worked weaving correctly, the yarns will cross evenly and remain at the same depth. A "smocking" effect means that you have pulled the yarns too tightly. It is better for the yarns to be woven too loosely than too tightly.

### STRANDING
If you have worked stranding correctly, the yarns will be running evenly across the back of the work at the same tension as the knitting.
Puckering indicates that you have pulled the yarns too tightly.

## SEAMS

Your pattern will usually set out the order of seaming: normally the shoulder seams are joined first if you have to pick up stitches to make the neck band. There is a choice of two methods, the edge-to-edge seam and the backstitch seam.

An edge-to-edge seam is useful on lightweight knits because it is almost invisible and forms no ridge.

A backstitch seam is stronger and firmer and is suitable for all garments but it forms a ridge.

### EDGE-TO-EDGE SEAM

Place the pieces to be joined edge-to-edge with the "heads" of the knit stitches locking together. Match the pattern pieces carefully row for row and stitch for stitch. Using the main yarn, sew into the head of each stitch alternately.

### BACKSTITCH SEAM

Place the pieces to be joined together with their right sides facing. Carefully match pattern to pattern, row to row and stitch to stitch. Sew along the seam using backstitch sewing into the centre of each stitch to correspond with the stitch on the opposite piece. Sew 6mm in from the edge of the knitting.

## INCREASING

### INCREASE 1 (Inc 1)

### IN A KNIT ROW

Knit into the front of the stitch in the usual way. Without discarding the stitch on your left-hand needle, knit into the back of it, making two stitches.

### IN A PURL ROW

Purl into the front of the stitch in the usual way. Without discarding the stitch on your left-hand needle, purl into the back of it, making two stitches.

## DECREASING

### KNITTING TWO STITCHES TOGETHER (K2 tog)

### IN A KNIT ROW (K2 tog)

Insert your right-hand needle through the front of the first two stitches on your left-hand needle. Knit them together as a single stitch.

### IN A PURL ROW (P2 tog)

Insert your right-hand needle through the front of the first two stitches on your left-hand needle. Purl them together as a single stitch.

## FINISHING TECHNIQUES

Before pattern pieces are joined up, they are usually blocked and pressed to ensure a good fit. It's always a good idea to check the yarn band for any special instructions. The pieces are blocked when dry and are pressed with a cloth.

### BLOCKING

Garment pieces need blocking, or putting into shape before they can be joined up. Cover a table with a folded blanket and a sheet. Using rustless pins, "block" the pieces wrong-side out to the correct measurements. Be careful not to stretch or distort the fabric and make sure that all the rows run in straight lines.

### PRESSING

After blocking, the garment pieces are usually pressed in position. Use a warm iron and a cloth on wool. Lay the iron on the fabric and lift it up, do not move it over the surface. Do not remove any of the pins until the work has cooled and dried completely.

Ribbing should be lightly stretched and pinned before ironing. Use a heavy cloth and remove the pins in order to adjust the fabric while it is still warm.

# Embroidery

## SWISS DARNING

### WORKING HORIZONTALLY

1  Secure the embroidery yarn at the back of the work and bring your needle out to the front of the work at A. Insert the needle at B, under the base of the stitch above, and bring it out at C.

2  Insert the needle at D and emerge at E ready to embroider the next stitch.

### WORKING VERTICALLY

1  Secure the embroidery yarn at the back of the work and bring your needle out to the front of the work at A. Insert the needle at B, bringing it out at C.

2  Take the needle under the head of the stitch below and emerge above it at D, ready to form the next stitch.

## SATIN STITCH

For best results, work horizontal straight stitches. The stitches should fit closely together, giving a very smooth surface and straight outside edges.

## FRENCH KNOT

Holding thread down with left thumb, encircle thread twice with needle. Then twist needle back to arrow and insert it close to starting point. Pull through to back before repositioning for next stitch.

## ADDING BEADS AND SEQUINS

Bring the needle out through the eye of the sequin and thread on a small bead, then insert the needle back through the eye of the sequin and pull tight so that the bead rests firmly over the eye, securing the sequin.

## CHAIN STITCH

Loop the working thread under the tip of your needle and hold it down with your left thumb while you pick up some of the ground fabric in each stitch. The needle is inserted into the same hole from which it has emerged.

To make a leaf shape, bring out your needle and insert it into the same spot bringing it out with a loop under the needle. Take it over the loop so that you make a small tying stitch to anchor it.

## BACKSTITCH

Work in small, even stitches by first making a stitch forwards and then a stitch backwards.

## STEM STITCH

Work the stitch with the thread kept on the same side of the needle. For a wider effect, insert the needle into the ground fabric at a slight angle. The greater the angle, the wider the effect.

# Bear Wear

## SWEATER INSTRUCTIONS

### MEASUREMENTS

| | |
|---|---|
| To fit chest | 22 (24,26,28,30)in |
| | 56 (61,66,71,76)cm |
| Actual chest measurement | 24 (26,28,30,32)in |
| | 61 (66,71,76,81)cm |
| Sleeve length | 12 (14,15,16,17)in |
| | 31 (36,38,41,43)cm |

### MATERIALS

Sirdar Country Style double knitting wool as found with each adventure in **Bear Essentials.**
1 pair of 3¼mm (No.10) needles
1 pair of 4mm (No.8) needles
2 buttons (optional)
2 15mm safety goo-goo eyes (or embroidery thread)

### TENSION

12 sts and 15 rows measure 5cm (2in) over stocking stitch on 4mm (No.8) needles (or size needed to obtain this tension)

### ABBREVIATIONS

k = knit; p = purl; k1b = knit into back of stitch; st st = stocking stitch; st(s) = stitch(es)

### WORKING NOTES

The **Front** is worked by following the appropriate chart (see **Working from charts, p.54**). All odd-number rows are knit rows worked from right to left, all even-number rows are purl rows worked from left to right, forming stocking stitch. The Back is worked by following the chart for the main background colours only, leaving out the motifs (see **Bear Essentials,** and photographs of sweater backs, pp.54–5).

The yarn for large blocks of colour should be carried up the work, not along the back, the yarn for smaller areas of colour should be woven in. See working with colours, pp.59 and 60.

### FRONT

With 3¼mm (No.10) needles and appropriate colour(s) for rib (as given under **Bear Essentials** for each pattern), cast on 72 (78,84,90,96) sts and work 12 rows in twisted rib as follows: k1, p1, *k1b, p1, repeat from * to end of row. Change to 4mm (No.8) needles and work stocking stitch following the chart for colour changes. Begin at row 1 for size 30, row 11 for sizes 26 and 28 and

row 21 for sizes 22 and 24.
**For the crew neck style,** work the neck shaping as indicated by leaving the centre 10 (10,10,12,12) sts on a stitch holder. Finish each side separately dec 1 stitch each side of neck edge as indicated on chart. Work to end of chart following shoulder shapings for appropriate sizes.
**For the slash neck,** omit the neck shaping and work over all sts to start of shoulder shaping, ending with a row on wrong side. Change to 3¼mm needles and appropriate colour, knit 1 row then work 7 rows twisted rib over all sts. Cast off right across in rib.

### BACK

Work rib as for Front in the same colour(s). Continue in st st following the chart but leaving out all motifs, working in background colours only, changing from one to another as on the Front of individual pattern (see photograph of sweater backs pp.54–5).
**For the crew neck** omit front neck shaping. When shoulder shapings are done leave remaining 24 (24,24,30,30) sts across back neck on a stitch holder.
**For slash neck** finish back exactly as for front.

### SLEEVES

With 3¼mm (No.10) needles and appropriate colour for sleeve rib (see **Bear Essentials**), cast on 37 (39,41,43,45) sts and work 12 rows twisted rib as for Front. On last row of rib increase 13 sts evenly across. Change to 4mm (No.8) needles and work in stocking stitch, increasing each end of the 5th and every following 6th row until 70 (74,78,82,88) sts, *at the same time* following instructions and colour changes of individual pattern. Continue until sleeve measures 30 (36,38,41,43)cm, 12 (14,15,16,17)in or length required. Cast off loosely with a 4mm (No.8) needle.

### NECKBAND

For crew neck only. With rights sides together, sew one shoulder seam. With 3¼mm (No.10) needles, knit 24 (24,24,30,30)sts across Back, pick up 26 (28,28,28,30)sts down side of neck, knit 10 (10,10,12,12)sts from stitch holder, pick up 26 (28,28,28,30) sts up other side of neck: 86 (90,90,98,102)sts. Work 6 (6,6,8,8) rows of twisted rib, knit 1 row, then work 6 (6,6,8,8) more rows of twisted rib. Cast off loosely with a 4mm needle.

### FINISHING

Block and press (see page 61). Using brown thread and backstitch embroider the bear's body – creases, paws, neck – as indicated on the pattern chart. Either attach two 15mm safety eyes to bear's face, or embroider two eyes in place. Using black wool, work the nose in satin stitch and the mouth in backstitch. Work any further embroidery as given on **Bear Essentials** following charts. Sew on decorative buttons as required.

### ATTACHING SAFETY EYES

Push the eye through the knitting, then push the backing firmly in place.

### EMBROIDERING EYES

With oddment of white yarn embroider larger circle in satin stitch. Then, using, oddment of black yarn, make a smaller circle in satin stitch.

**To make back of head** With 4mm (No.8) needles and brown yarn, cast on 18 sts and work in st st for 18 rows, cast off. With wrong sides together, sew this to the back of the bear's head to encase the back of the eyes. If you like, add a little stuffing to make the face stand out.
**Crew neck version** Sew the other shoulder seam. Fold the neckband in half to the wrong side and sew loosely in place.
**Slash neck version** Oversew shoulder edges together for 3–5cm (1½–2in) from outside edges, leaving central neck opening.
**Both versions** Sew in sleeves. Darn in all the ends from the motifs and changes of colour. With a fine backstitch, sew up side and sleeve seams, oversewing over ribbing. Press again if necessary, avoiding safety eyes.

**Washing instructions** If you are using safety eyes and buttons, the sweaters should be hand washed and not tumble-dried. Otherwise, they can be washed on a wool setting and left to dry. Press under a dry cloth, avoiding eyes and buttons.

# Useful Information

## USEFUL ADDRESSES

In case of difficulty in obtaining the yarn, write to:
**Sirdar PLC**, Flanshaw Lane, Alverthorpe, Wakefield WF2 9ND, West Yorkshire.

**Hayfield Textiles Ltd.,** Glusburn, Keighley BD20 8QP, Yorkshire.

The safety eyes are obtainable in yarn shops or by mail order from **Pick 'n Choose,** The Craft People, 56, Station Road, Northwich CW9 5RB, Cheshire, refer to 15mm "goo-goo" eyes.

Kits are available for Patterns Nos. 3, 10, 13, 15 and 16 which include the yarn required for the size, buttons, goo-goo eyes and stuffing.
Send an S.A.E. for a price list to "Mo", **Creative Designs in Knitwear,** 7 Mossfield, Cobham KT11 1DF, Surrey.

## ACKNOWLEDGEMENT

Dorling Kindersley Ltd. would like to thank Mothercare for lending clothes for the photographs.

## ALTERNATIVE YARN CHART

| SIRDAR COUNTRY STYLE DOUBLE KNITTING | HAYFIELD GRAMPIAN DOUBLE KNITTING |
|---|---|
| Parchment (404) | Ulva (005) |
| Cream (411) | Cream (015) |
| Naturelle (409) | Coffee Cream (079) |
| Parasol Pink (413) | Clover (043) |
| Lupin (429) | Hyacinth (031) |
| Saxe (440) | Bluebell (014) |
| Corona Yellow (460) | Daffodil (073) |
| Majestic Mink (482) | Fudge (017) |
| Dark Chocolate (439) | Burnt Brown (016) |
| Warm Cinnamon (495) | Praline (128) |
| Eucalyptus (426) | Mint (041) |
| Blue Haze (407) | Skye (004) |
| Stormcloud (472) | Silver Birch (023) |
| Fiery Sunset (469) | Lilac Cream (082) |
| Chalky Grey (430) | Silver Birch (023) |
| Chalky Blue (464) | Forget-Me-Not (042) |
| White (412) | White (011) |
| Silver Cloud (434) | Silver Birch (023) |
| Black (417) | Black (024) |
| Royal (449) | Royal (040) |
| Flamenco (442) | Scarlet (012) |
| Honey Bird (453) | Aqua (124) |
| Warm Cerise (462) | Calypso (121) |
| Carolean Jade (467) | Shamrock (075) |
| Oriental Jade (481) | Peacock (117) |
| Pink Cloud (476) | Dapple Grey (100) |